With respect to Country and all
children
who walk gently upon it.

First published 2026

Printed in Australia

ISBN

Acknowledgement Of Country

We promise to look after the land,

We promise to look after the water,

We promise to look after the trees,
And all the buzzing bees.

We acknowledge the Bunurong mob,

And all our non indigenous friends,

And promise to walk gently,

So the Earth shall live and breathe.

Journeys On Country
Poem Stories and Hand and Body Actions for children

By T. Bellaburra

Contents:

Me On Country

learning through movement and senses

My body feels Country.

The sun wakes me up to tell me it's morning.
I jump out of bed to say, "Hey, good morning."

My feet love to feel the grass under them
as I jump and jog
while the sun shines on me.

My hands do handstands.
I balance on one leg.

I pick up a leaf
and feel it softly with my hands.

I see a little flower
and smell its sweet smell with my nose.

I hear the birds singing,
and my ears listen carefully.

My body on Country
helps me understand.

Then I sit down
and cross my legs
to feel the breeze.

Country gives me
all and everything I need.

Hand and Body Actions: Me On Country

.Learning Through Movement ad senses.

My body feels Country.
Place both hands on your chest and take a slow breath.

The sun wakes me up to tell me it's morning.
Stretch arms up high like the rising sun.

I jump out of bed to say, "Hey, good morning."
Do a gentle jump and wave hello.

My feet love to feel the grass under them
Stamp feet softly on the ground.

as I jump and jog
Do small jumps or a gentle jog on the spot.

while the sun shines on me.
Lift your face and arms toward the sky.

My hands do handstands.
Reach hands down toward the ground or bend forward.

I balance on one leg.
Stand on one foot with arms out wide.

I pick up a leaf
Pretend to pick something up from the ground.

and feel it softly with my hands.
Gently rub fingers together.

Hand and Body Actions: Me On Country

.Learning Through Movement ad senses.

I see a little flower
Make circles with fingers and look closely.

and smell its sweet smell with my nose.
Bring hands to nose and sniff gently.

I hear the birds singing,
Cup hands behind ears and listen.

and my ears listen carefully.
Stand still and tilt head slightly.

My body on Country
Place hands on your heart.

helps me understand.
Nod slowly.

Then I sit down
Lower body slowly to the ground.

and cross my legs
Sit comfortably with legs crossed.

to feel the breeze.
Gently move arms side to side.

Country gives me
Open arms wide.

all and everything I need.
Hold still and take a quiet breath.

Homes on Country

This is a nest for a fairy wren.

This is a hive for a bee.

This is a cocoon for a moth.

And this is a house for me.

This is a cave for a bat.

This is a hole for a wombat.

This is a web for a spider.

And this is a house for me.

Hand and Body Actions: Homes on Country

This is a nest for a fairy wren
Hands gently cupped together, palms facing up, like a small nest.

This is a hive for a bee
Hands as clenched fists, either side by side or one resting on top of
the other.

This is a cocoon for a moth
Hands together in a prayer position, fingers pointing upward.

And this is a house for me
Arms lifted above the head, fingertips touching to make a roof shape.

This is a cave for a bat
Arms lifted above the head, making a big round cave shape.

This is a hole for a wombat
One hand resting on the hip as the hole.
The other hand moves like a wombat going into the hole.

This is a web for a spider
Both hands held in front of the face, fingers spread wide to show a web.

And this is a house for me

Arms lifted again above the head, fingertips touching to make a roof shape.

We All Have Friends On Country

Two little echidnas tapping on their knees.

Two little koalas stamping with their feet.

Two little seagulls squawking loudly at me.
Squawk, squawk.

Two little wombats digging holes, you see.

Two little blue tongues poking their
 tongues at me.
Blop, blop.

Two little possums playing peekaboo
 with me
 Peekaboo.

Two little bilbies softly hop around.
Two little magpies swooping all around.

Two little cockatoos clapping with their
 wings.
Clap, clap.

We all wave goodbye.
We shall see you all real soon.

To all our friends on Country,
we love you and care for you.

Hand and Body Actions: We all have friends on Country

Two little echidnas tapping on their knees.
Tap hands gently on knees.

Two little koalas stamping with their feet.
Stamp feet slowly on the ground.

Two little seagulls squawking loudly at me.
Open arms like wings and make a gentle squawking sound.
Squawk, squawk.

Two little wombats digging holes, you see.
Use hands to pretend to dig in the ground.

Two little blue tongues poking their tongues at me.
Stick tongues out playfully and say blop, blop.

Two little possums playing peekaboo with me.
Put hands over eyes, then open them and say peekaboo.

Two little bilbies softly hop around.
Do small, gentle hops on the spot.

Two little magpies swooping all around.
Stretch arms out and swoop in slow circles.

Two little cockatoos clapping with their wings.
Clap hands together, pretending they are wings.

We all wave goodbye.
Wave hands slowly.

We shall see you all real soon.
Point to eyes, then reach arms forward.

To all our friends on Country, we love you and care for you.
Place hands on heart, then open arms wide.

Tiptoe on Country
A Little Counting Yarn

Five little kookaburras
flutter in the sky.

Four sandy crabs
scurry scurry by.

Three little wombats
waddle to their hole.

Two sweet echidnas
sniffing with their nose.

One sleepy snake
curled up so small.

Tiptoe, tiptoe,
we tiptoe away.

We care for Mother Nature,
who loves us as we play.

Hand and Body Actions: Tiptoe on Country

Five little kookaburras flutter in the sky.
Flap arms gently like wings. Look up and softly flutter fingers above head.

Four sandy crabs scurry scurry by.
Bend knees slightly. Wiggle fingers like crab claws. Shuffle sideways across the room.

Three little wombats waddle to their hole.
Place hands on hips. Waddle slowly side to side. Crouch down low at the end.

Two sweet echidnas, sniffing with their nose.
Hold hands like little paws in front. Take two gentle sniffing breaths. Wiggle noses and smile.

One Sleepy snake curled up so small.
Slowly curl your body down. Hug knees in close. Rest your head quietly.

Tiptoe, tiptoe, we tiptoe away.
Stand up softly. Tiptoe lightly around the room. Hold a finger to your lips for quiet steps.

We care for Mother Nature, who loves us as we play.
Place hands on your heart. Open arms wide like a gentle hug. Finish standing still and calm.

Sounds on Country

With our hands we shape a billabong,
a quiet place where water rests.

With our arms we go round and round,
just like the wind with its gentle sound.

With our feet we stomp the ground,
like thunder rolling all around.

Our faces shine like a sunny day,
then rain and pout on a cloudy day.

We peep like cheeky possums do,
hiding behind a branch or two,
then jump out fast to say peekaboo.

Our bodies move with Country's
 song,

The wind, the rain, the land, that's
where we belong.

Hand and Body Actions: Sounds on Country

With our hands we shape a billabong
Children cup their hands to make a round, still shape
.

A quiet place where water rests
Hands stay still and low, bodies become calm and quiet.

With our arms we go round and round
Arms move slowly in big circles.

Just like the wind with its gentle sound
Children sway softly side to side like the breeze.

With our feet we stomp the ground
Children stomp their feet gently on the spot.

Like thunder rolling all around
Stomp a little louder, then fade back to soft.

Our faces shine like a sunny day
Big smiles, hands lifted like warm sunshine.

Sounds on Country

Then rain and pout on a cloudy day
Fingers wiggle down like rain, faces turn soft and cloudy.

We peep like cheeky possums do
Children cover their eyes or hide behind their hands.

Hiding behind a branch or two
Peek through fingers like branches.

Then jump out fast to say peekaboo
Children pop up and say "Peekaboo!
"

Our bodies move with Country's song
Children move freely to the sound.

The wind, the rain, the land, that's where we belong
Hands on heart, then touch the ground.

Tiny creatures on Country

Snail
Slowly slowly, so very slowly,
She journeys up the trail.
Slowly slowly, so very slowly,
The snail moves soft and free.

Ants
Quickly quickly, so very quickly,
The ants scurry scurry.
Quickly quickly, so very quickly,
They scurry to their holes in the ground
.

Caterpillar
Wiggly jiggly, wiggly jiggly,
Chomping all the way.
Wiggly jiggly, wiggly jiggly,
Caterpillars are on their way
.

Chrysalis
Spinning spinning, spinning spinning,
They're spinning their chrysalis.
Spinning spinning, spinning spinning,
So quiet, yet restless.

Butterfly
Magic, magic, yes magic,
This does happen on Country.
Magic, yes magic, let's wait and breathe,
Until a beautiful butterfly pops out to see,
Then flies off to discover Country.

Hand and Body Actions: Tiny creatures on Country

Take your time between each creature and follow the children's pace.

Snails
Encourage the children to creep their hands slowly up one arm, moving as slowly as they can, like a snail travelling along a trail. Pause for a moment.

Ants
Guide the children to move their fingers quickly around their face and head, scurrying about like busy ants. Then invite their hands to travel back down to the ground and into their little holes. Pause again.

Caterpillar
Encourage the children to wiggle and jiggle their bodies from side to side, moving along slowly as if they are caterpillars making their way across a leaf. Pause.

Chrysalis
Show the children how to roll their arms gently around each other, spinning slowly, as if they are forming a chrysalis. Gradually slow the movement and come to stillness. Rest quietly for a moment.

Butterfly
Invite the children to take a slow breath in and out. Then gently open their arms and flutter them softly, imagining they are butterflies flying away to explore.

Move slowly, allow space for pauses, and let the children's movements guide the flow.

Tracks on Country

Footprints on Country everywhere I see.
Some belong to animals and some belong to me.

Big ones and small ones.
Tracks zig and zoom.
A waddling little wombat
and a hopping kangaroo
.

Tiny little bird prints tip tap in a row,
and a lizard leaves a tail line
everywhere it likes to go.

A bandicoot's soft hopping
like dots upon the sand,
and high up in the branches
are the handprints of a possum's hand.

Big three toed emu tracks
stride across the land,
and the tiny echidna dig marks
make patterns in the sand.

Every track I follow
shows stories old and new.
Country holds each gentle step,
maybe mine or maybe yours too.

Hand and Body Actions: Tracks on Country

Footprints on Country everywhere I see.
Look down at the ground and point around you.

Some belong to animals and some belong to me.
Point outward, then point to yourself.

Big ones and small ones.
Stretch arms wide, then make yourself small.

Tracks zig and zoom.
Move finger in zigzag lines through the air.

A waddling little wombat and a hopping kangaroo.
Waddle side to side, then do small hops.

Tiny little bird prints tip tap in a row
Tap fingers lightly in a line.

And a lizard leaves a tail line everywhere it likes to go.
Drag one hand slowly along the ground or through the air like a tail.

Hands & Body Actions: Tracks on Country

A bandicoot's soft hopping like dots upon the sand
Do gentle, quiet hops in place.

And high up in the branches are the handprints of a possum's hand.
Reach arms up high and place hands against an imaginary tree.

Big three toed emu tracks stride across the land
Take long, slow steps.

And the tiny echidna dig marks make patterns in the sand.
Use fingers to gently scratch or draw patterns.

Every track I follow shows stories old and new.
Walk fingers forward like following a path.

Country holds each gentle step.
Place feet firmly on the ground and pause.

Maybe mine or maybe yours too.
Point to yourself, then open hands toward others.

Shadows on Country

When the sun is rising
and the morning feels new,
I look on Country
to see if my shadow's there too.

I run outside smiling,
the breeze on my face,
to see the shadows dancing
around my place.

Look at the magpies
as they strut around,
searching for food
on the soft, warm ground.

And guess what?
Their shadows come too,
walking beside them
in everything they do.

Then all of a sudden
the shadows all hide,
as a cloud makes a shadow
that spreads far and wide.

I push the cloud's shadow
and I push it away,
and all my friends on Country
have their shadows laughing again today.

Hand and Body Actions: Shadows On Country.

When the sun is rising and the morning feels new
Stretch your arms up slowly like the sun rising and take a deep breath in.

I look on Country to see if my shadow's there too
Look down at the ground and wiggle your fingers or feet to notice your shadow.

I run outside smiling, the breeze on my face
Jog gently on the spot• Fan hands softly near face

To see the shadows dancing around my place
Move your arms side to side and let your body sway like dancing shadows.

Look at the magpies as they strut around
Walk with proud, slow steps and keep your hands by your sides like wings.

Searching for food on the soft, warm ground
Look down and pretend to peck gently at the ground.

Hand and Body Actions: Shadows On Country

And guess what? Their shadows come too
Point to the ground beside you and look surprised

Walking beside them in everything they do
Walk slowly and let one hand follow the other like a shadow.

Then all of a sudden the shadows all hide
Freeze your body or crouch down low.

As a cloud makes a shadow that spreads far and wide
Stretch your arms wide and move slowly like a cloud passing over.

I push the cloud's shadow and I push it away
Use gentle pushing movements with your hands and step forward softly.

And all my friends on Country have their shadows laughing again today
Jump or twirl lightly and move with joy.

a

Yarning About Animals on Country

Where's a wallaby?
There's a wallaby.
Boing, boing, boing.

Where's an emu?
There's an emu.
Zoom, zoom, zoom.

Where's a bat?
There's a bat.
We fly at night.

Where's a platypus?
There's a platypus.
Splashing in the
creeks and streams.

Where's a koala?
There's a koala.
Munch, munch, munch.

Where's a dingo?
There's a dingo.
howl, howl, howl,

Where's a possum?
There's a possum.
Tiptoe on the branches.

Where's a goanna?
There's a goanna.
Creep, creep, creep.

Hand and Body Actions
Yarning About Animals on Country

Where's a wallaby?
Look around and shade eyes.

There's a wallaby
Point gently.

Boing boing boing
Small jumps on the spot.

Where's an Emu?
Look ito the distance.

There's an Emu.
Stand tall

Zoom zoom zoom
Run lightly on the spot

Where's a bat?
Look up to the sky.

There's a bat.
Raise arms wide.

We fly at night.
Flap arms wide..

Hand and Body Actions
Yarning About Animals on Country

Where's a platypus?
Look down near the ground.

There's a platypus.
Point to the water.

Splashing in the creeks and streams.
Make a splashing motions with hands.

Where's a Koala?
Look up into the trees.

There's a Koala.
Point up high.

Munch, munch, munch
Pretend to chew slowly with hands to mouth

.Where's a dingo?
Look across Country.

There's dingo.
Point with excitement.

How, howl, howl.
Cup hands around mouth and lift head to howl.

Hand and Body Actions
Yarning About Animals on Country

Where's a Possum?
Look up into the branches.

There's a possum.
Point up towards the branches.

Tiptoe on the branches.
Tiptoe quietly in place with gentle feet and hand movement..

Where's a goanna?
Look down on the ground.

There's a goanna.
Point low to the ground.

Creep, creep, creep.
Bend knees and creep forward slowly,

Sea Country

On the beach we feel the sand,
soft and warm, come take our hand.

We jump the waves and wade around,
and listen to the ocean sound.

On the beach we love to find
feathers, rocks, shells of all kinds.

We watch the gulls fly round and round,
feel the breeze that pushes clouds.

On the beach we hug the ground,
and listen to the soft sea sounds.

On the sand, on the shore,
Sea Country is a home for all.

Hand and Body Actions: Sea Country

On the beach we feel the sand
Wiggle fingers downwards and rub hands together like sand.

Soft and warm, come take our hand
Rub arms gently, then hold hands or reach out.

We jump the waves and wade around
Make small jumps, then walk slowly on the spot.

And listen to the ocean sound
Cup hands to ears and gently sway.

On the beach we love to find
Look down and pretend to search with hands.

Feathers, rocks, shells of all kinds
Pretend to pick up small treasures and place them in your hand.

We watch the gulls fly round and round
Stretch arms out wide and move them slowly like wings.

Feel the breeze that pushes clouds
Lift arms and softly move them across the sky.

On the beach we hug the ground
Crouch down and wrap arms around knees or touch the earth.

And listen to the soft sea sounds
Place a hand to the ear and breathe slowly.

On the sand, on the shore
Sweep one hand across the ground, then look out to the horizon.

Sea Country is a home for all
Open arms wide in a welcoming gesture.

Hope you enjoyed your Journey.

Created for early childhood and primary learning.
Shared journeys on Country.

About the Author

T. Bellaburra has created Journeys on Country, poem stories that gently guide children to connect with Country in a fun, engaging, and meaningful way. Each poem is paired with simple actions and movements to support learning through the body, imagination, and joy, while respectfully embedding Aboriginal perspectives.

Connecting children to Country helps them understand the natural world around them. Through these poems, children are invited to learn why animals, insects, plants, and landscapes are important, how everything has a purpose, and how all living things are connected. This understanding nurtures care, respect, curiosity, and responsibility for the world they live in.

T. Bellaburra's love for nature and Country sits at the heart of everything in this book. Children are our future, and with deep respect, this book is shared for the love of Country, wellbeing, and healthy connections to the earth.